Photographs
Colin Jea...

Front cover painting by:
Julie Stooks

*We would like to thank the following for
permission to photograph their stock:*
**Hansards Pet Centre, Romsey
Kevin Curtis
Small Mammal Breeding Centre,
Denmead**

Your First

GERBIL

CONTENTS

your first gerbil

Kingdom Books is an imprint of T.F.H. Publications   Printed in England.

INTRODUCTION

Look up the word 'gerbil' in your dictionary or encyclopedia. The word is pronounced 'jur-bil' and comes from the Latin *gerbillus* meaning 'little jerboa'. Under the entry 'jerboa', you will learn that this is a jumping desert rodent found in the remote, arid regions of Asia and Africa. However, this is not much help, since neither the gerbil nor the jerboa is a native of the Western Hemisphere.

MONGOLIAN GERBILS

The gerbil you will own is probably the Mongolian gerbil, which originated in northeastern China and eastern Mongolia. Throughout this book the word 'gerbil' is used to mean 'Mongolian gerbil'.

In the family tree of animals, true gerbils are members of the order Rodentia, suborder Myomorpha, super-family Muroidea, family Cricetidae, sub-family Gerbillinae, genus *Meriones*, and species *unguiculatus*. Thus, the scientific name *Meriones unguiculatus* is used to denote Mongolian gerbils. Meriones was a Greek warrior who wore a helmet decorated with boars' tusks; *unguiculatus* comes from a Latin word meaning 'fingernail'. This 'tooth-and-nail' concept seems very inappropriate for such a small, peaceful animal!

Mature gerbils are smaller than rats but larger than mice. They are about 10cm long, and their furry, tufted tails are about the same length again. Their weight seldom exceeds 115g. The fur on their backs and tails is a tawny or reddish brown, with black outer tips and a grey undercoat. The underside of the body is light grey or creamy white. The head is broader and more foreshortened, and with smaller ears than either a rat or mouse. The eyes are large, dark, and bulge slightly. The hind legs are elongated and the forefeet are relatively small; each foot has five toes with long, thin nails. Thus, the gerbil has evolved with protective colouring suitable for a desert life and with limbs adapted for every sort of activity. Their general colouring, appearance, postures and actions are similar to some squirrels.

GERBILS IN THE WILD

Little is known of the gerbil's life in the wild, where it is called the desert rat, sand rat or jird. Gerbils are burrowing animals which live far from sources of water, eating seeds, grains, grasses, roots and plants found in their desert environment. They are active during the day and at night to a lesser extent. A colony of gerbils lives in a tunnel, two to three metres long, with several entrances. It extends several metres underground, and usually has tunnels branching off at different levels. Various chambers along the main tunnel serve as rooms for nesting and food storage.

GERBILS AS PETS

Scientists first began to study gerbils in the 1950s. The animals were easy to care for and had gentle dispositions so, by 1965, they were well established as very desirable pets. They are not cuddly, but seem to enjoy being handled and will not bite unless mistreated. Their friendliness, curiosity and quick, squirrel-like movements are fascinating to adults and children alike.

Gerbils have simple requirements for housing, food and water. They are clean, odourless and easy to keep that way. They are healthy and hardy and make very little noise. They do not hibernate in winter or become lethargic in summer, and are active during the day. They do not try to escape but are relatively easy to recapture if they do get loose.

Gerbils seem happiest and most active when kept in mated pairs, so you must expect to cope with babies. Alternatively, you could obtain a pair of gerbils beyond breeding age which still can provide you with plenty of interesting activity and friendly behaviour.

A White Mongolian gerbil.

BEHAVIOUR

The gerbil has several specific habits and customs which are interesting to observe. These are part of the animal's daily life and you should look at what your pet is doing so that you understand it better.

ACTIVITY CYCLE

The gerbil's life is one of cyclic activity, alternating periods of intense activity with short naps throughout the day. When awake, it darts to and fro, investigating everything going on around it. It nibbles at food continually. It burrows into the bedding, gnaws on available material and makes nests. The gerbil concentrates so hard on these activities that it is easy to understand why it needs the occasional rest.

A gerbil often stretches out its forefeet and yawns just like a cat or a dog. Soon it is in such a deep sleep that, except for its breathing, you may wonder whether it is still alive. In warm weather, it may push away the bedding to lie on the bare cage floor. It sleeps in every position imaginable: curled up on its side, stretched out on its stomach, or even flat on its back! In cool weather, gerbils often sleep bunched together. They like to tuck their heads down between their hind feet and curl their tails around their bodies, and look just like balls of fluff.

When the gerbil is resting or asleep, you should not disturb it. This would be interfering with its natural way of life, and it might become irritable - like a child who misses his nap.

CURIOSITY

When you approach the gerbils' cage, they will always come to see what new food or plaything you have for them to try out. They are eager to investigate almost any toy or object you offer to them: tubes, toy bridges or ladders, vehicles, baskets, boxes, pieces of paper or building blocks. (As the gerbil is a compulsive chewer, make sure that none of these objects can harm your pet.) This interest in a new thing is short-lived, and curiosity soon makes them ready to explore something new. Their curiosity is so great that a hungry gerbil put into a maze with food at the end stops to explore every 'dead end' passage before it reaches its goal.

In captivity, the gerbil has little chance to learn fear from experience. Sudden movements or noises may startle gerbils, especially young ones, but this reaction seems to be one of surprise rather than fear. Generally, they do not seem to be afraid when they encounter strange objects, people, noises or other pets. Therefore, you must be careful when you let your

The gerbil has an enquiring nature, and enjoys exploring its surroundings.

gerbil come into contact with other animals. Some dogs and cats can be trained to ignore gerbils, but most will regard them as a tasty meal or a new toy.

BURROWING

In the wild, gerbils spend a lot of their time burrowing to make their homes and scratching for food among the desert scrub and grass. They dig rapidly with their short forefeet, and use their hind legs to kick the excavated material behind them. Sometimes they also use their heads to push things out of the way. The gerbil's forefeet have sharp nails, so eventually it will burrow through cardboard or scratch wood or plastic. However, I do not know of any instance where a pet owner has been scratched so hard that the skin is broken.

Occasionally, you may look into the gerbil cage and think that you have lost your pet. The chances are that the 'missing' animal has burrowed completely beneath the bedding material. Rap lightly on the cage and a whiskered face will pop up, ready for the next adventure.

GNAWING

The gerbil's incisors continue to grow throughout its lifetime. If they are too long or too short, the gerbil could not survive for long. In captivity this is seldom a problem. If necessary, you can provide a block of wood for tooth exercise, although the hard food in the diet usually suffices. Gerbils will attempt to gnaw or chew on almost any available material: bedding, nest material, paper, cardboard, cloth, wood, bone, plastic and even metal. This is a normal part of their everyday life.

MOVEMENT

One of the gerbil's talents is to jump up using its hind legs and this has earned it the nickname 'pocket kangaroo'. In the wild, gerbils can jump nearly a metre if they need to. Young gerbils can use their hind legs for jumping by the time they are weaned.

When a cage full of youngsters is suddenly startled, it looks like a box of jumping beans scattering in various directions! Some gerbils leap straight up when startled. They can jump forwards, backwards, sideways, or even turn completely around in mid-air. Older gerbils do not jump so often, although they still have the ability. In captivity, even unconfined gerbils seldom jump more than about 45cm horizontally or 15cm vertically.

Usually, gerbils move about on all four feet, with their short forefeet providing balance and support. From time to time, they pause to sit or stand on their hind legs, like squirrels. This is the position they prefer to be in to eat and drink. To satisfy their curiosity, gerbils stand erect, stretch upwards, and even lean backwards slightly while still maintaining their balance. The tail balances the gerbil while it is sitting, standing or landing after a leap. During a jump, it may act like a rudder to guide the animal through the air.

Gerbils can climb wire mesh vertically with no difficulty, but they cannot hang upside-down from a mesh cage roof for long.

NOISES

These pets are relatively quiet animals. Their only vocal sound is a faint, high-pitched 'chee-chee', more like the cheeping of a bird than the squeaking of a rodent. You will not hear very much noise, unless a litter of young is present or the parents have a brief argument.

From weaning age, most gerbils make a sound on the cage bedding or floor by rapidly drumming or thumping their hind legs. This staccato 'ta-ta-tat' may be a warning signal, like the thumping of a rabbit's foot. It seems to mean 'Attention!' and may be repeated by other gerbils within hearing. It also seems to indicate excitement in new surroundings or at mating time. The rapid burrowing or scratching action of the forefeet against the cage floor or walls also produces a characteristic rustling or rasping sound.

GROOMING

Gerbils like to be clean, and keep themselves well groomed. Using their forepaws and tongue, they 'scrub' their faces, heads, ears, bodies and tails

The gerbil holds its food in its front paws so that it can pick at it delicately.

like cats, often grooming each other. These actions promote cleanliness, stimulate the skin, prevent matting of the fur, and help keep the coat glossy. Because gerbils come from very dry climates, their skin produces certain natural oils to combat dryness. Dampness or high humidity may result in ruffled coats, which the animals take care of by grooming and by rolling in dry bedding material.

The pallid gerbil blends in well with its surroundings.

SELECTION

By the age of one month the chances are that a healthy gerbil will go on to lead a full and healthy life. However, it is advisable to add a few weeks to this age just to be sure, and get your gerbils when they are about six to eight weeks old. At this age they will be fairly hardy, not too nervous, and their appearance and actions will give you much pleasure.

Gerbils are most active and seem to be happiest when kept in sexed pairs. Two mature males or females may fight if kept together, especially if they were raised in different families. The same is true for mixed groups of older males and females. If you are able to keep only a single gerbil, either sex seems to be equally satisfactory, but you must be sure to give your pet lots of attention and provide toys to keep it active and contented.

APPEARANCE

Look for those animals whose movements and actions are quick and bobbing, like a squirrel. They should be alert: an unexpected movement on your part should startle them.

The body should be moderately filled out and firm-looking; a too-fat appearance may be due to old age or overfeeding. The fur should be relatively long, soft and glossy. The nose and head should be somewhat foreshortened rather than long and thin. The ears should be fairly small, not too rounded, and should stand erect. The eyes should be relatively large but not too bulgy, and be bright and twinkling.

It is difficult to tell what the tail will turn out like, as it is only one-fourth as long as the gerbil's body at birth and almost the same length as the body when the animal is fully grown. However, look for a kink in the tail or a stubby tail with a blunt tip, even it it is tufted, which may be the result of injury.

Fighting may produce a partly closed eye, a scab on the mouth, a lump on the head or nose, or sore spots on the rump. Be sure to examine the feet and nails to see that they are in good condition.

Bald spots could mean a dietary deficiency. Frequent scratching of the fur may indicate the presence of external parasites. Runny eyes or nose, a wet bottom, skin ulcerations, unusual lumps, or sore places may signal a disease or a condition that could be beyond your care.

Pet shops offer a variety of cages that are suitable for housing gerbils. Cages can be made of wood, sheet metal, glass, plastic, wire mesh or grid, or combinations of these materials.

CAGES

Gerbils seem to thrive better in cages with solid bottoms. A floor space about 25 x 50cm or 40 x 40cm is adequate for a pair plus a litter of offspring. The standard large hamster cage, small animal cage, 50-litre aquarium, and even some of the large bird cages sold in pet shops may meet these requirements. The cage height should be 20-25cm to allow for the gerbil's habit of eating or drinking from a sitting position, plus some stretching

A wild pygmy gerbil looking out of its burrow.

space. Each type of cage has advantages or disadvantages in durability, sanitation, weight and security. Metal, plastic and glass are better as they are easier to clean. Wood is the cheapest but also the least durable and sanitary. Gerbils can and will gnaw prominent wood surfaces, and they can scratch wood and plastic surfaces to some extent.

Normally your gerbils will not jump high enough to escape from an aquarium or open-top cage, but it is best to provide some form of lid to keep out intruders and still allow ventilation. These covers can be made of wire mesh or bought in standard sizes from your pet shop. The spacing of the cage wire mesh or grid should be about one centimetre; this will prevent your gerbil from rubbing its nose raw during its attempts to gnaw the metal.

The cage sides and ends should be solid and reach a height of 10cm above the base. This has several advantages: it reduces the scattering of the bedding material which the gerbils throw about as they burrow, prevents the accidental loss of newborn gerbils through the mesh or grid openings, and provides protection against draughts.

BEDDING

Provide bedding material to a depth of 5-10cm on the cage floor. The gerbils will arrange it to suit their needs, depending on the temperature and their own desires. This material should be clean, absorbent, dustless and non-toxic. Pine shavings, coarse sawdust, wood shavings, husks, grass, leaves or any commercial litter material will be adequate.

CLEANLINESS

Gerbils are perhaps the cleanest of all pet animals. Their body wastes amount to so little that you need to change the cage bedding material only every two or three weeks. If a litter of young arrives when you normally clean the cage, you can wait until weaning time to change the bedding. Of course, you should change the bedding if it becomes soaked with spilled water or if it is obviously soiled. Bedding may have to be changed more frequently in warm weather than during cool weather.

When you remove the soiled bedding, give the cage a quick scrape and sweep. Several times a year you should use a solution of disinfectant suitable for pets to clean the cage and utensils. Be sure to dry and air the cage thoroughly before returning the animals to their home.

When your gerbils are put back in their cage, they will burrow into the new bedding and work busily to rearrange it. This is a good time to put a small amount of hay or tissue paper in the cage for the gerbils to shred into nesting material, which will last until the next bedding change.

Because the gerbils are so clean and lack any odour, there is no reason why they should not be kept in almost any room of your house.

FURNISHINGS

Gerbils will make the best use possible of any floor space as a playground. Even so, most gerbils enjoy using an exercise wheel, which provides a good outlet for their excess energy. A food container, a standard water bottle, some toys or playthings and a piece of wood for gnawing complete the furnishings of the gerbils' home.

TEMPERATURE AND HUMIDITY

In its native environment, the gerbil stays comfortable by retreating to the burrow during the heat of the day or the chill of the night. In captivity, its requirements are nearly the same as those of your home: about 21-27°C and 40-60% relative humidity. Temperatures as low as 10°C can be tolerated as long as you provide ample bedding and nesting material. Gerbil cages can be left outdoors, provided that you supply adequate protection against rain, sun, wind and predators. The best way to achieve this is to place the cage inside a garage or garden shed.

Gerbils kept in an aquarium or in transparent plastic cages must be protected from exposure to direct sunlight. The sun's rays, plus the insulating and possibly magnifying properties of the cage walls, could raise the inside temperature to 40°C or more, which may be fatal.

ESCAPES

The burrowing, scratching and gnawing activities that gerbils carry out do not necessarily mean that they are anxious to escape. These actions form an instinctive part of their daily life. It is more likely that a gerbil will escape by accident, so here are some methods of recapture.

Often an escaped gerbil is quite willing to return to its home voluntarily, especially if you put some sunflower seeds near the cage. If you remain still, it may wander back to you after it has explored its surroundings.

Because gerbils love to explore tunnels, one successful means of recapture is to place a cardboard or plastic tube near an escaped gerbil, using some seeds or bedding as bait if necessary. When it enters the tube, cup your hands over the ends, pick up the tube and return the gerbil to its cage. Alternatively, you can lay a baited jar or other empty container on its side and pick it up once the gerbil is inside.

You can also employ a trick used to recapture hamsters. Place a bucket in the room where your gerbil is hiding and make the room escape-proof. Make a series of steps from the floor up to the bucket lip, using wood blocks or bricks. Put some seeds and bedding on the steps and in the bucket; you can also put the escaped animal's mate inside the bucket (ensure that the bucket is high enough that neither of them can jump out). By the next morning your escaped gerbil should be safely in the bucket.

Always make sure that your gerbil is in a secure place, or it is bound to go exploring.

The gerbil's ability to stand on its hind legs has led to its nickname of 'kangaroo rat'.

FEEDING

To maintain your pet's health and to satisfy its energy needs, you must provide a balanced diet that meets all the requirements for good gerbil nutrition.

DRY FOOD

Gerbil or hamster mixes, available from pet shops, are specially formulated to satisfy a gerbil's dietary needs. A mix contains an assortment of grains such as wheat, corn, oats and barley, as well as sunflower seeds, pumpkin and other small seeds, peanuts and vegetable flakes. This dry food forms the bulk of your pet's diet. As a treat, give your gerbil plain biscuits, old dry bread and similar food. You will soon learn how much food to give. Generally, about a tablespoonful per day per adult, and about half that for a young animal, is enough.

There is no hard-and-fast rule when to feed your pets. Perhaps the most convenient time is in the late afternoon. Your gerbils will soon learn when to expect their food, and will become very active when they hear the sounds associated with their feeding routine. They do not hoard food and, except for sunflower seeds, they do not overeat.

Sunflower seeds are the gerbil's favourite treat. It is fascinating to watch a gerbil deftly hold and manipulate a seed in its forepaws, slit the shell with its sharp incisors, extract and devour the kernel, then discard the husk and reach for another. Most gerbils have mastered this trick by the time they are three weeks old. Do not give too many of these seeds, though, as they contain a considerable amount of fat, and your pet might develop a waistline problem!

GREENS

Supplement the dry food with greens several times a week to supply additional vitamins and minerals. You can offer small amounts of fresh lettuce, celery, carrots, kale, parsley, parsnips, apple peel, grass, dandelion, alfalfa and similar foods. Although gerbils are not as susceptible to diarrhoea as some other small rodents, greens should be given only in limited quantities to avoid the risk of intestinal upsets.

Taking the above into account, the gerbil's diet allows you considerable possibilities for variation. Individual animals may show certain food preferences, and you will enjoy testing their tastes every now and again. Hay should be available at all times, as this helps with digestion, promotes a glossy coat and also provides the gerbil with some bedding material.

Gerbils should have bright, shiny eyes, like this black Mongolian.

FOOD CONTAINERS

You can serve your gerbil's food in a heavy, shallow saucer or plate that cannot be tipped over, but a better alternative is a food container that attaches to the side of the cage. Food served like this is less likely to become soiled by droppings and bedding material.

WATER

The gerbil's desert heritage means that it does not need to drink very much, but fresh water should be available to it at all times. Do not use dishes or plates, as the animal's burrowing actions will upset or contaminate the water and there is a risk that young gerbils might drown in the container. Additionally, gerbils prefer to drink from a sitting position.

A standard watering bottle is fairly cheap, can be attached easily to the cage with a spring or wire clip, and helps to ensure the water stays clean. Be sure to choose one with a stainless steel spout. To provide a convenient drinking height, and to prevent the bedding from acting as a wick to drain the bottle, locate the bottle so that the end of the spout is several centimetres above the top of the cage bedding. If your gerbil cage is an aquarium or other solid-walled container, you can bend a length of wire to support the inverted watering bottle inside one corner of the cage.

HOLIDAY TIME

Gerbils travel well, but you will probably decide to leave them at home when you go on holiday. You can leave them unattended for up to two days because they need so little care, but it is wise to ask someone to check on them in case of accidents. Before you leave, provide fresh bedding, a container holding plenty of dry food, and a bottle of fresh water. Give each gerbil a suitably-sized chunk of raw carrot as this supplements the dry diet and provides an emergency water supply. Double-check to make sure that the cage is escape-proof and located out of direct sunlight and draughts. If you are going to be away for more than a couple of days, you must arrange for someone to replenish the animals' food and water and change the bedding.

When you first bring your gerbils home, offer them food and water, but let them rest for a day before you handle them. This gives them some time to recover from their journey and get used to their new home.

The best way to pick up a gerbil is to place one or both hands, cupped with palm up, underneath its body before lifting it up. At first, let it walk onto your open palm before picking it up; this will prepare it for the experience. Later you can lift it with a gentle, but fairly rapid, scooping motion. Don't grasp its tummy - it may feel trapped and struggle to escape.

A gerbil has a good sense of height and, when lifted above any solid surface, seldom jumps or climbs down without considerable deliberation. However, it is a good idea to hold your pet in the palm of one hand and hold the base of its tail with the other hand to avoid accidental falls. When gerbils are on a table, they recognise that they should not venture beyond the edge. However, they might skid off it or simply forget that it is there, and you must be alert to prevent such accidents.

Your pets will enjoy climbing up your arm and perching on your shoulder, but do not make any abrupt movements that could result in them falling. They like to crawl in and out of collars, pockets or hoods but make sure that they do not burrow or chew enough to damage your clothing.

The gerbil's long tail acts as a balance whether it is sitting, standing or jumping.

TAMING AND TRAINING

Generally a gerbil will bite hard only if it is handled badly - being chased, teased, squeezed, etc. Of course, if you hold your finger directly in front of its mouth, a hungry gerbil might nip you. If a bite results in broken skin, you should apply disinfectant. Whatever animal you keep, you should make sure that you are protected against tetanus.

Use the gerbil's gentleness, curiosity, friendliness, activity cycle and food preferences to achieve successful taming and training. A gerbil's

A pair of gerbils greeting each other.

The long tail will come off if the gerbil is handled in the wrong way, so owners must always take care how they hold their pets.

intelligence seems high for its size; for example, it learns to avoid certain situations or conditions about 10 times faster than white rats. You yourself must be patient and understanding so that your pet develops trust and confidence in you.

Young gerbils may be jumpy and nervous for a few weeks so keep the training sessions brief. Keep in mind the gerbils' activity cycle. If you interrupt or prevent a needed rest period, they may become irritable. Be slow, calm and deliberate in your movements and speech. Let the gerbils become accustomed to you gradually and, remember, even your hand may seem like a giant to them! At feeding time, let the animals eat some seeds or bits of lettuce from your fingers. While they are eating, gently scratch their heads, ears or backs; this will help them get used to your touch. During later training sessions, offer various treats as a reward, especially if you are trying to teach some simple tricks.

As you progress, let your gerbils out of the cage so that they can have some freedom in a secure area such as a large box, a table top or even a bath. Gerbils enjoy these outings, especially if you provide interesting objects for them to explore. They will probably return voluntarily to their cage for food or rest, or you can coax them back or pick them up.

Make a gerbil playground. All you need is a large box, two or more gerbils, and some toys that gerbils like. Almost any cardboard or wood box will do, or you can use a metal tub, plastic sandbox or a rigid wading pool. I can guarantee that you will enjoy the sight of your gerbils as they play.

Do not allow gerbils the run of your house as they might get lost or injured. However, you can give them the freedom of one room occasionally. Make sure that the room is escape-proof to keep gerbils in and dogs and cats out. You will have to watch your step (literally) because gerbils often come near your feet, either out of curiosity or because of some need for physical security.

You can take your gerbils outdoors, weather permitting, but they should be confined to a box or some other enclosure. If they escape from your control, they could become victims of domestic animals or birds, predators or poisonous sprays. Do not take nervous gerbils outside and very active, excitable animals may prove too unruly to handle. Many gerbil owners advise a strictly indoor life for their pets.

In captivity gerbils breed best in mated pairs. Two or more females kept with a single male will result in failure or disaster; either there will be no productive matings or the females may bully the male to death. If a female gerbil loses her mate, she is reluctant to accept a new one, and may completely refuse to be with him.

MATURITY AND REPRODUCTION

Sexual maturity occurs between the ages of nine and twelve weeks. Generally the sexes can be distinguished at three weeks. The male's body has a tapered bulge (usually tufted) near the base of his tail, and there is a scrotal pouch. The female's rump is more rounded and her genital opening is close to the anal opening. As a rule, mature males are somewhat larger in size and weight than females.

Two gerbils put together when still quite young usually pair off quite happily. Once the pair is established, the male can be left safely with the female at all times, including during the nursing of a litter.

You can provide a wood or metal nesting box with a suitable doorway, but most gerbils seem content to build nests from cloth, paper or leaves, which they shred into strips with their teeth and forepaws. Both the male and the female join in the nest building.

Gerbils breed throughout the year; there is no apparent seasonal variation. Mating often occurs immediately after the arrival of a litter, and sometimes during the nursing period. The gestation period is about 24 days. Unless you are a careful observer, you may not be able to detect that the female is pregnant without weighing her.

Because gerbils are naturally so quiet, the first indication of a new litter may be the high-pitched calls of the newborn babies. Most litters are born during the night or early morning, although very occasionally they arrive during the afternoon. Birth is relatively uncomplicated and painless, taking approximately an hour even for a large litter. Since no help is needed from you, it is advisable to leave the female undisturbed at this time.

The litter size ranges from one to ten, with an average of four or five young, and will probably contain an equal number of males and females. Most females will bear their first litter by the time they are six months old. About one-third of all females may have their first litter at three to four months. The female's reproductive life can last up to 20 months, although usually it is over by 14 months.

Above: A female black gerbil watches over her day-old young.
Below: The gerbil baby is now ten days old.

TIPS FOR SUCCESSFUL BREEDING

As a pet owner, probably you will not be able to match some of the favourable conditions achieved by commercial breeders. Nevertheless, if you keep to the following suggestions, you should have an excellent chance of success in breeding your gerbils.

1. Ensure that you provide sufficient cage space, bedding and nesting material.
2. Keep your gerbils' diet relatively high in protein and low in fat.
3. Provide adequate privacy: a cage with one or more opaque sides may help.
4. Place the cage where there is a minimum of disturbance from household noise and traffic.
5. Do not handle your gerbils in the evening.

YOUNG GERBILS

Newborn gerbils are naked and pink, blind, toothless and deaf. They are little more than 5cm long and weigh about 3g. The percentage of live births is high and cannibalism is rare. If the female does eat her young, it may be because they have died from a lack of milk due to some dietary deficiency; you may be able to prevent this by giving the mother some evaporated milk during pregnancy and nursing.

The male can be left with the female and the litter, although his duties usually consist only of occasionally herding the young back to the nest and sitting on the nest to help keep the babies warm.

The first week of life is critical. Do not handle the animals during this period as such disturbances might cause the mother to trample, smother or desert her young.

When the young stray from their nest, which can happen at an early age, the mother usually returns them by scooping them with her forefeet, pushing them with her nose, or even by picking them up bodily in her mouth. These measures do not seem to cause any harm. Then she will busily re-shape the nest to keep all her babies warm and secure. If the litter is large, some females keep their young in two nests, dividing the nursing time about equally. You can offer some bits of bread crusts soaked in milk, but this is not necessary for a nursing mother if you feed her on a balanced diet and make drinking water available.

A pair of pied white spot gerbil babies. Their eyes are not yet open.

By the age of three days, the young can crawl, albeit in rather an ungainly manner. At five or six days the ears are open. By two weeks the babies are fully covered with fur. In a few more days, the incisors come through and the babies are ready to explore their world by gnawing. At the same time, their eyes begin to open and generally their movements are more coordinated.

At three weeks, gerbils weigh about 14g. They can eat solid food, drink from a watering bottle, climb wire mesh, stand up, jump and thump their hind legs. Now is the time when they should be weaned. This may seem a tender age for weaning, but the animals adjust easily, and it is important to remove them from the nest to avoid overcrowding and strain on the parents should another litter arrive in a few days. (It should be the exception, not the rule, to allow the adults to mate again straight away.)

Weanlings can be sexed and placed in separate cages or kept in a community group until they are about eight weeks old. At this age, they should be separated to prevent inbreeding. When you pair off the gerbils, it is a good policy not to put brother and sister together. The closest relationship that I recommend is second cousin. The young can be housed in smaller quarters than adults, but you should allow about 130 sq cm per animal.

For the first week after weaning, you can put some unsweetened breakfast cereal in with the gerbils' regular solid food; this is easily handled and the animals seem to like it. You can also offer some milk-soaked bread crusts. Position the watering bottle so that the spout is where the young can reach it and they will learn how to use it quickly.

Some litters may have one or two runts, caused by nursing difficulties or dietary deficiencies. Often these gerbils grow to normal size and catch up with their litter-mates. If the runts are bullied by their brothers and sisters, you should isolate them to allow them to develop in peace.

When the gerbil's coat consists of more than one colour, it is called 'pied'.

The fat-tailed gerbil stores fat in its tail, which it lives off when it cannot find other food.

HEALTH

The gerbil is relatively healthy and hardy and will remain so with a minimum of care from its owner. You can expect its normal life span to be from two to three years.

With regard to illness, prevention is better than cure, because the successful treatment of some diseases of small animals is almost impossible. Preventive measures include proper diet, fresh water, strict cleanliness, sufficient cage space and ventilation, and protection against dampness, extreme temperatures and draughts.

Diarrhoea and other intestinal disorders seem to be rare among gerbils. If such illnesses occur, they could be related to the diet - perhaps the gerbils have eaten too many leafy greens, or taken in some contaminated food.

Colds and similar conditions are seldom a problem but their symptoms include listless activity or droopiness, runny eyes or nose, and lack of appetite.

Balding, eye injuries, body sores and external parasites may sometimes affect the gerbil. Always consult your veterinary surgeon before treating the animal yourself.

Some vets are better than others at treating small animals. I would advise you to visit the surgeries in your area and find a vet that you can trust with your pet.

FURTHER INFORMATION

If you want to find out more about gerbils and get in touch with fellow enthusiasts, contact the National Mongolian Gerbil Society at the following address:

The National Mongolian Gerbil Society
Secretary: Jackie Roswell
373 Lynmouth Avenue
Morden
Surrey SM4 4RY

GERBILS
Paul Paradise
ISBN 0-87666-927-5
KW-037

For the gerbil keeper and admirer looking for specific information on the proper care of the animal this book offers sensible and accessible recommendations to the fancier.

Hardcover: 128 x 204mm, 95 pages,completely illustrated with full-colour photos and drawings.

GERBILS:
A Complete Introduction
Mrs M Ostrow
ISBN 0-086622-267-7
CO-018

All the basics of good care, management and breeding are presented in tandem with colourful photos of this playful little rodent. The different colour varieties are illustrated in photographs. This book brings the beginner a complete and useful approach to animal husbandry.

Hardcover: 128 x 204mm, 128 pages. Full-colour photos, plus helpful line drawings.

PROFESSIONALS' BOOK OF GERBILS
Bob Bernhard
ISBN 0-86622-669-9
H-909

This comprehensive book is refreshingly complete and well written. The author concentrates on providing information that readers will be able to put to good use and benefit from; both the beginner and the experienced gerbil keeper will find this an indispensable companion to gerbil care and breeding.

Hardcover: 128 x 204mm, 160 pages, 75 full-colour photos.

THE PROPER CARE OF GERBILS
Anmarie Barrie
ISBN 0-86622-187-5
TW-106

This book, aimed primarily at the novice, introduces the reader to all aspects of gerbil keeping. Topics include housing, feeding, taming, handling, breeding and health care.

Hardcover: 128 x 204mm, illustrated throughout with colour photographs, 256 pages.